THE DEATH PENALTY

CAPITAL PUNISHMENT IN THE USA

David K. Garfield

© 2015

DISCLAIMER

TABLE OF CONTENTS

INTRODUCTION

The simplest definition of the term capital punishment is; the execution of a defendant after having been found guilty in a trial for a criminal offence, that in the eyes of the law warrants this most extreme of punishments. The term "death penalty" refers to the sentence itself, and not to the execution which is termed "capital punishment". This linguistic sleight of hand is important because these days the pronouncement of this punishment is rarely followed by an immediate carrying out of the sentence, in fact the average time between sentence and execution is often measured in years, this fact alone contributes to the ongoing controversy surrounding the death penalty in North America.

This book is intended to give the reader both an overview of the history of capital punishment, globally and in the United States, but also hopefully an insight into why the practice appears to be so ingrained into the American penal system. The reader will learn how capital punishment has evolved through the 20th century, and also how the methods of execution differ, i.e. how capital justice is dispensed. In Chapter 3 you will be given details of where the executions take place; this information has been expressed in table form with the relevant sources listed underneath. The remaining chapters of the book are concerned with how the death penalty fits into the broader social dynamic of the United States; discussing both the objective and subjective arguments for and against capital punishment in the modern world. These arguments can then be applied by the reader to all nations, including the United States which employs the death penalty.

Discussing Capital punishment can be disturbing, so some of the descriptions contained in this book are deliberately detached and clinical. Capital punishment is not a static subject; in fact it is a dynamic and fluid discipline of social science. As a result it is important that the reader appreciates that any statistics quoted are correct as at March 2015, and any factual information included is potentially subject to rapid change in different states across the US; consequently the reader is advised to confirm any details included in this book as legislation changes. The basic foundation of this book is however based on a variety of reputable primary and secondary sources, which can be perused via the presented hyperlinks and sources listed.

If you wish to explore issues pertaining to race, class, and gender in more detail; then you are advised to follow up with the resources listed in the 'Further Sources' section, as well as the hyperlinks within the book itself.

This document is not designed to present a case for, or against capital punishment, and it is also not an exhaustive text. It is simply meant to give the reader an overview of the subject as well as suggest further sources of independent research, allowing the reader to come to an informed decision.

Finally, from a legal perspective it is important to stress that this is not an authoritative text, the legislative nuances of Capital Punishment are best left to professional lawyers and other legal professionals.

CHAPTER 1 - A CONCISE HISTORY OF CAPITAL PUNISHMENT

The practice of Capital punishment has existed amongst the human race since the mid to late Bronze Age. In ancient (4000–221BC) and imperial (221BC-1911) China the most common methods of execution were:

- Quartering; either by dismemberment or attachment to chariots
- Boiling alive
- Slow slicing
- Strangulation

However, if you had the means you could rescind these penalties by payment of a large fine. Clearly therefore, the higher an offender's position in society the more likely it was that the said person could bargain for his or her life. For offences such as treason, the death penalty would also apply to the extended family of the accused; their contacts; their liaisons; and any other person they were even suspected of being acquainted with. For this crime the favored method of killing was the torture known as slow slicing. These more extreme methods of execution were not banned in China until 1905.

Approximately 4000 years ago, King Hammurabi who ruled over the state of Babylon from 1792 to 1750 BC, set down 282 rules which if broken would incur some penalty. During his rule the Babylonians expanded their kingdom to such an extent that by the end of his Life King Hammurabi ruled over much of what is now present day Iraq. These 282 statutes were carved into diorite (a form of igneous rock) and intended to help facilitate and maintain the cohesion of the kingdom. Within the edicts, 25 crimes were set down as punishable by death, yet murder was not one of them. The law was unequal in the extreme, should a slave or commoner steal from a temple or shrine then capital punishment was almost certain. The method of execution would involve inflicting intolerable pain (torture) on the individual concerned. Execution methods included stoning, dismemberment, crushing by elephant, disemboweling and burning, as well as the skinning and/or gouging out of the eyes of the condemned. Should a wealthy individual commit the same crime then payment of a heavy fine or a tribute would normally suffice. Additionally, even if the penalty was still death, a much less painful and degrading method was usually applied, such as beheading. Ignoring the obvious brutality of these 282 codes, they are historically important because put simply, they are the first true example of a society that believed an accused was innocent of the offence they were charged with, until proven guilty.

Such a premise is meaningless if, as in 7th century Athens, all crime, no matter how trivial, was punishable by death. For example, in the Athens of the time you could be executed for stealing grapes. In fact the word Draconian is derived from a set of laws set down by the ancient Greek lawmaker Draco in about 620BC. Clearly such extreme measures render the law itself meaningless and as a result within about 40 years all of these laws were abolished except for those pertaining to murder. The empire of ancient Greece was a thriving province of the Roman Empire; however a crucial defeat at The Battle of Corinth in 146BC firmly set in motion a series of events that resulted in the complete assimilation of the province of Greece into the Roman Empire. By the time of its collapse in about the mid-4th century AD, over 80 crimes carried the sanction of capital punishment.

At about this time the most common method of execution in post Roman Britain was to throw the condemned person into a bog, or another form of quagmire, where they would drown. By the 10th century AD, hanging from the gallows was the preferred method of dispensing capital justice. Execution was almost always accompanied by torture and/or mutilation. I say "almost", because once again if an individual had sufficient means, they could pay to bypass the torture and go straight to the beheading. Figures vary for the number of people executed on the orders of Henry VIII (1509-1547), but 72,000 is a generally accepted ball park figure. From 1532, the punishments included being boiled alive, in tar, oil or water; this was eventually outlawed in England in 1631 however in other parts of the world this still appears to continue today. By the turn of the 17th century over 220 crimes in what is now called the UK, were considered capital offences. They included stealing in excess of 40 shillings from a private residence, or faking your tax return. By the 1840's most of these former capital crimes were no longer classed as such. The abolitions occurred against a backdrop of frenzied debate on the necessity of the death penalty as a whole. By 1869, eleven parliamentary debates that resulted in votes on capital punishment had occurred. At this time, public hangings were banned, and simultaneously imprisonment for debt was abolished. Capital punishment was abolished (except for treason) in the UK in 1969, and as of 1998 in the UK, no criminal act has been considered a capital offence. In addition to this the European human rights act stipulates that no EU country which has signed the act can under any circumstances reinstall the death penalty. The impact of this decision on those US states which continue to carry out the death penalty was significant, and is discussed in more detail in Chapter 7. There are currently some political forces in the UK that would like to reverse some of the current EU legislation, a move which would doubtless be welcomed by advocates of capital punishment in the US.

For the 13 former colonies of the emerging US, the use of the death penalty was directly influenced by practices in Europe. In other words the death penalty travelled with those who emigrated; with Britain perhaps being the dominant influence. Arguably, this could be considered a principal reason for the reluctance in removing capital punishment from US legislation.

The range of acts which fell under the designation "capital" varied greatly among the colonies. The first person to be executed was an officer known as <u>Captain George Kendall</u> who was one of the original founders of Jamestown, in the colony of Virginia. He was executed by firing squad on 1608 on a charge of "spying for Spain".

Perhaps reminiscent of the draconian laws in 1612, the governor of Virginia Sir Thomas Dale brought forward the <u>divine, moral and martial laws.</u> Under these statutes one could be executed for stealing fruit or engaging in trade with the Native American Indians.

The religious dimension to the death penalty was equally strong, in the colony of New York a person could be executed for denying the existence of "the one true god". By 1776 the degree to which capital punishment was actually used varied hugely across the 13 colonies, although each colony generally considered the same type of offences as capital crimes and early laws were drafted with an appropriate scripture from the Old Testament. Capital punishment could be applied to those found guilty of:

- Murder and premeditated murder
- Rape and statutory rape
- Perjury in a capital trial
- Sodomy and bestiality
- Manslaughter
- Poisoning
- Adultery and idolatry
- Slave and horse theft
- Treason or another denial of the Kings rights

The principal method of execution at this time was by hanging.

There were however some colonies that didn't fully adhere to these rules; in South Jersey the death penalty did not exist for any crime, and in Pennsylvania the death penalty was only sought for murder and treason. Massachusetts was another anomaly as they only sought capital punishment for murder; sodomy; treason; rape; arson and burglary.

The law concerning the death penalty in the US was first seriously reviewed between the years 1776-1780, this period become known as first great reform era and was heavily influenced by the 1767 English publication of "On Crimes and Punishment" by an Italian jurist named Cesare Beccaria. The book concludes that there is no justification for the state to execute its citizens and that a lengthy prison term is a far bigger deterrent. Thomas Jefferson and others across the colonies began to propose that the death penalty should only be applied for treason and murder; initiatives such as these had a profound impact on the use of capital punishment. For instance, in a legislative debate in Virginia in 1800, the proposed bill limiting capital punishment was only defeated by one vote. This did not however stop the number of offences which were considered capital from steadily dropping. For instance by 1794 in the state of Pennsylvania; only premeditated murder carried a mandatory death penalty for the guilty person. The abolitionist position at this time centered on two basic arguments; one moral and the other rooted firmly in practicality and perception. The moral argument concerns the unacceptability of the state sanctioned killings, and the practical concerns the degree to which such acts work as a deterrent to committing capital crimes in the first place. This question continues to present the foundation of the death penalty debate today, in which we ask "is the death penalty itself a sufficient deterrent when measured against the prospect of a long (if not lifetime) prison sentence in a harsh and brutal institution?" Intertwined with this position is the question of trust in the judiciary and law enforcement agencies themselves, as well as the assumed natural need for "satisfaction or retribution" on the part of the relatives of the victims. Overall, the fundamental questions to ask are whether or not execution is the best deterrent for the most heinous crimes, does it work, and is the evidence upon which the conviction is decided absolutely sound?

The next major reform that occurred was the transfer of executions from being a public spectacle, to something that was done in private; namely public hangings became illegal. The hangings themselves had become significant events, sometimes attracting tens of thousands of people. Executions were therefore progressively carried out in purpose built rooms known as execution chambers away from the public eye. These execution facilities were constructed in dedicated wings of state penitentiaries, which in popular jargon have since became known as "death row".

Over the two decades between 1830 and 1850, a total of 15 states banned public hanging; however it was not until the 20th century that the final public hanging took place in the execution of the convicted rapist Rainey Bethea in Kentucky in 1936, who was hung in front of thousands of people. During the US civil war opposition to the death penalty abated but only due to the focus on the issue of slavery in the Southern States. With this in mind, it is important to remember that although many

US states at the time did abolish the death penalty (except for treason), many more did not, especially if the crime was carried out by a slave.

A further issue in the history of the death penalty presented itself in 1838 when many states began to apply a discretionary, as opposed to mandatory approach to death penalty sentencing. Prior to this date no consideration was given to the circumstances in which the crime had taken place, in fact from 1863 many Northern US states had abolished their mandatory death penalty laws entirely and instead used their own discretion when crimes were considered particularly abhorrent.

Since the 16th century no fewer than <u>15000 persons</u> have been executed for a designated capital offence in the US alone. It is important to stress that the US is not the only country in the world to execute its citizens, but it is the only advanced western economy to do so. Taken as a whole, the US is ranked 5th in the world for the number of executions with, in sequence; Saudi-Arabia; Iraq; Iran and China constituting the remaining four nations.

As of 2015, 18 US states have abolished the death penalty but with approximately <u>55% of Americans</u> in support of capital punishment for murder, the controversy surrounding the use of the death penalty continues to roll.

Chapter 2 - Capital Punishment in the United States Since 1900

Between the years 1895-1917, a period known as the <u>second great reform era</u> began. This occurred against the backdrop of the emergence of the electric chair as the dominant method of execution.

In 1897 congress passed various bills which further reduced the number of federal capital offences. Overall, by the turn of the 20th century the number of capital crimes had effectively been reduced to murder and kidnapping.

In 1907 the state of Kansas abolished the death penalty entirely for all offences, and following on from that between 1911 and 1917, a further 8 states abolished the death penalty except in the case of rape. A number of other states also came very close to passing equivalent laws on ending capital punishment.

The pendulum of death penalty acceptance, swung against the abolitionist movement between 1917 and 1955 when the states of Oregon, Washington and Arizona, all reinstated the death penalty before the end of 1920. In addition to this by 1924 death by gassing had been introduced as a new method of dispensing capital justice, and following the execution of <u>Mrs. Eva Dugan</u> in 1930 (convicted of murder), whose sentence of death by hanging was an unmitigated disaster (the hangman miscalculated the drop distance and the head of the condemned was unceremoniously torn from her body) there was a further uptake of electrocution and gassing as the preferred method of killing capital prisoners.

During the first decades of the 20th century, opposition to the death penalty was centered on the executions of convicted prisoners as opposed to the punishment itself. This was particularly true of the period covering 1920-1940; in part because of the impact of <u>prohibition</u> on murder statistics, which recorded a <u>staggering</u> 78% increase when compared to pre-prohibition rates, but also because of the position many criminologists and social commentators took at the time; they argued that the death penalty was a profound mechanism by which to control (if not deter) extremely undesirable behavior. From 1920 to 1940 the number of inmates executed reached an average of three figures per year. For example; in the 1930's an average of 167 prisoners were put to death every year, almost all by electric chair. This figure represents the highest in United States history and is considerably higher than the current average of 48 (by lethal injection), with the overwhelming majority occurring in the states of <u>Texas and Oklahoma.</u>

In the 1950's, during the hysteria of McCarthyism and the witch-hunting of any people who were deemed un-American, the then governor of Texas (Allan Shivers) attempted to pass a bill that would make membership of the Communist Party an offence punishable by death. Surprisingly the number of executions actually dropped at this time, in fact only 715 prisoners were executed in the 1950's compared to 1300 in the 1940's.

In 1957 Hawaii and Alaska abolished capital punishment, rapidly followed in 1958 by Delaware, although it was reinstated in Delaware in 1961. By the mid-1960's public support for capital punishment was recorded at 42%, the lowest in US history. Against this backdrop capital punishment was removed from the statute of Oregon in 1964, and in the following year the principal capital crimes in the US were designated as murder, rape, armed robbery, kidnapping, sabotage, espionage (spying) and burglary. In the same year, the states of Vermont, Iowa, West Virginia and New York, followed by New Mexico in 1969 became the latest jurisdictions to abolish capital punishment.

A pivotal moment in this aspect of modern American history was the suspension of Capital punishment across the whole of the United States by the Supreme Court in 1972. The explanations for this occurrence are complex and would be best answered by a legal expert, but essentially it was due to some details found within the 8th (prohibiting cruel and unusual punishment) and 14th (which holds that all citizens of the United States are treated equally) amendments. At this time the juries in capital cases had total control and were able to compel the judge to impose a capital sentence. In what became three landmark cases, the Supreme Court voted 5 to 4 in favor of the fact that capital punishment in its current form was arbitrary, did not match the crime, and was therefore effectively unconstitutional. As a result of this on the 29th June 1972, 40 capital offences were declared null and void, resulting in 629 death row prisoners having their sentences commuted. It must be remembered that the vote was not against capital punishment as such, but more concerned with how it was carried out. Over the next four years capital states in North America rewrote their legislation so that it eliminated the issues raised in Georgia Vs Furman. A whole range of intricate and complex legal wrangling ensued, employing terms such as "*the unconstitutionality of unguided jury discretion*" and the introduction of "*bifurcated trials*", i.e. once an offender is found guilty of a capital crime, a second trial is set to decide whether the convicted person should be executed.

In anticipation of a reversal of the Supreme Court decision, by 1975 a total of 30 states had reinstated death penalty laws and over 200 prisoners were on death row. A year later in 1976 a whole swathe of reforms to death penalty legislation were accepted by the Supreme Court; and on July 2nd in what became known as the Gregg decision, Capital punishment was reinstated by a vote of 7-2. At the same time however the Supreme Court held that sentencing someone to death for the offence of the rape of an adult (if not resulting in death) contravened the 8th amendment and was therefore unconstitutional. The case of Coker Versus Georgia resulted in a situation whereby a convicted person can only be executed in certain states where the offence is not murder. Today, if a case gets referred to the Supreme Court a capital sentence can be overturned if the crime didn't result in murder.

Following this decision, although it was seemingly more difficult to gain a capital sentence, as of 1976 executions recommenced. On January 17th 1977, the moratorium on executions ended with the execution of the convicted murderer Gary Gilmore in Utah by firing squad.

It can be argued that the official four year hiatus and unofficial ten year hiatus in executions resulted in a death penalty backlash. By 1977 a total of 34 states including Oregon had new death penalty laws, and Oklahoma was the first state to pass laws allowing execution by lethal injection. The reasoning for this was as steeped in economics as it was on humanitarian grounds; electric chairs were, after all, expensive to repair and / or maintenance. Furthermore, the cost of building a gas chamber was hundreds of thousands of dollars, a fact that continues to be a challenge for those who wish to pursue this method of execution today (see Chapter 7). In comparison, in 2011 the cost of a lethal injection was only ten dollars per execution.

Although not officially sanctioned until 1977, proposals to execute capital offenders by lethal injection can be traced back to the 19th century and the invention of the hypodermic needle. The state of New York, (which at the time sanctioned executions) proposed that injections would be more humane than both hanging and the electric chair. The suggestion was rejected at the time on the basis that the populace may then associate the needle with administering death as opposed to saving lives. In addition to this, the fact that a lethal injection had be used by Nazi Germany as part of their mass killings of the sick, disabled, infirm, weak or otherwise incapacitated, was also another reason it was dismissed. Similarly, in the UK during the 1950's, proposals were made to carry out capital sentences by lethal injection, but they were immediately dismissed due to profound objections from the medical establishment. This sort of mindset simply does not exist in the mind of those who support capital punishment.

In 1977 Dr Jay Chapman, (a supporter of the death penalty) who was paradoxically the chief medical examiner in Oklahoma (although not registered as an anesthesiologist), first proposed carrying out capital punishment by administering three different drugs in a prescribed order, giving the state executioners an alternative to the electric chair. Furthermore, the use of the lethal injection meant that theoretically the punishment itself would be easier to carry out, and also easier for witnesses to view as the inmate being killed would not writhe, scream, combust or burn whilst dying.

After approval in Oklahoma in 1977, the first execution by lethal injection was carried out in Texas on December 2nd 1982. The prisoner, Charles Brooks Jr was found guilty of the kidnap and murder of an employee of a car dealership.

In states where alternatives to the lethal injection still exist, if prisoners don't express a preference for the method of their execution, the authorities will employ the lethal injection.

In 1994 there were 315 capital sentences handed down by US courts and 39 executions followed; in 1999 this figure was 98 and in 2013, 80 sentences were passed and 39 inmates were executed. In May of 2013, the state of Maryland abolished the death penalty, later the same year Texas carried out 16 executions and so far in 2015 it has carried out 5; this is significantly less than the 40 it carried out in 2000. These and other figures from the Death Penalty Information Center (DPIC) website seem to indicate that the use of the Death penalty is being questioned again, although there is no single reason for the decline and also no reason to presume that the use of capital punishment will definitely decrease in years to come.

In 2004 the state of New York rescinded the death penalty on constitutional grounds and applied it to the sole surviving inmate on death row. There have since been numerous attempts to restore capital punishment but hitherto all have failed.

In 2008 in another pivotal vote the Supreme Court voted 7-2 in favor of the use of lethal injection by the State of Kentucky. The appeal against the use of lethal injection on constitutional grounds was brought by the death row inmates Ralph Baze and Thomas Bowling, who had both been convicted of double murder. Arguably, Kentucky was not the best place to base such a decision as the Kentucky authorities had only carried out one execution.

In March 2009 and April 2012 respectively, the states of New Mexico and Connecticut both voted to abolish the death penalty. However the repealing of the act was not retrospective, therefore at the time of writing this, two people remain incarcerated on Death Row in New Mexico and 11 in Connecticut. On the 10th of November 2009 John Allen Muhammed was executed by lethal injection by the state of Virginia. His accomplice, Lee Boyd Malvo was sentenced to life without parole, they were convicted of killing at least 10 people (possibly as many as 27) in a three-week killing spree which ended in Washington DC. John Allen was the first prisoner to be executed after a de-facto 7 month moratorium on lethal injections after the Supreme Court judgement of 2008.

As of 2013 the majority of US citizens support capital punishment. However, the recorded level of 60% is significantly less than the 80% recorded in 1994. Additional polls which target different sectors of the population reveal that it is mainly older white Americans that support capital punishment. For reasons which should be relatively obvious; support amongst the young and ethnic minorities is significantly less. Such demographic considerations will undoubtedly have implications for the future of capital punishment in the US.

The current situation in North America is that of the 32 states which have capital punishment, 15 have not executed anyone since 2010. Furthermore, the states of Texas, Oklahoma, Florida and Virginia are responsible for almost two-thirds of all executions since 1976, with Texas carrying out 37% of the total.

Chapter 7 will explain how capital states are finding it increasingly difficult to carry out lethal injections as per the original stipulations of Dr. Chapman, and the final chapter summarizes the details of an upcoming crucial vote that is expected by the end of June 2015.

CHAPTER 3 - WHERE DO THE EXECUTIONS OCCUR?

There are currently still 32 states which carry the death penalty. The figures below are a collation of the current statistics of how those US states carry out the sentence, and the numbers of persons who have either been convicted, who are currently incarcerated on death row, or have been executed.

The figures concerning executions after 1976 are for those states which have not as yet abolished the death penalty, and the figures pertaining to executions between 1608 and 1976 are not limited to the modern scope of current capital crimes. They should not therefore be used to support the basis of an argument, either for or against capital punishment.

TABLE ONE - STATE BY STATE BREAKDOWN OF DEATH PENALTY STATISTICS

State	Capital Crime	Method of Execution	Number of executions after 1976	Number of executions between 1608 and 1976	Inmates on death Row as of October 2014
Alabama	Intentional murder with 18 aggravating factors	Lethal Injection, Electrocution	56	708	198
Arizona	First-degree murder, including premeditated murder and felony murder, accompanied by at least 1 of 14 aggravating factors	Lethal Injection, Gas chamber	37	104	123
Arkansas	Capital murder with a finding of at least 1 of 10 aggravating circumstances; treason	Lethal Injection, Electrocution	27	478	33

State	Capital Crime	Method of Execution	Number of executions after 1976	Number of executions between 1608 and 1976	Inmates on death Row as of October 2014
California	First-degree murder with special circumstances; sabotage; train wrecking causing death; treason; perjury causing execution of an innocent person; fatal assault by a prisoner serving a life sentence	Lethal Injection, Gas chamber	13	709	745
Colorado	First-degree murder with at least 1 of 17 aggravating factors; first-degree kidnapping resulting in death; treason	Lethal Injection	1	101	3
Delaware	First-degree murder with at least 1 statutory aggravating circumstance	Lethal Injection, Hanging	16	62	18
Florida	First-degree murder; felony murder; capital drug trafficking; capital sexual battery	Lethal Injection, Electrocution	90	314	404

State	Capital Crime	Method of Execution	Number of executions after 1976	Number of executions between 1608 and 1976	Inmates on death Row as of October 2014
Georgia	Murder with aggravating circumstances; kidnapping with bodily injury or ransom when the victim dies; aircraft hijacking; treason, **carnal knowledge of a female who is less than 10 presuming force**	Lethal Injection	57	950	90
Idaho	First-degree murder with aggravating factors; first-degree kidnapping; perjury resulting in the execution of an innocent person	Lethal Injection	3	26	11
Indiana	Murder with 16 aggravating circumstances	Lethal Injection	20	131	14
Kansas	Capital murder with 8 aggravating circumstances	Lethal Injection	0	57	10

State	Capital Crime	Method of Execution	Number of executions after 1976	Number of executions between 1608 and 1976	Inmates on death Row as of October 2014
Kentucky	Capital murder with the presence of at least one statutory aggravating circumstance; capital kidnapping	Lethal Injection, Electrocution	3	424	35
Louisiana	First-degree murder; treason, **aggravated rape of a child under 13**	Lethal Injection	28	632	85
Mississippi	Capital murder; aircraft piracy	Lethal Injection	21	351	49
Missouri	First-degree murder	Lethal Injection, Gas chamber	81	285	9
Montana	Capital murder with 1 of 9 aggravating circumstances; aggravated kidnapping; felony murder; aggravated sexual intercourse without consent; **second conviction for sexual intercourse without consent accompanied by serious bodily injury**	Lethal Injection	3	71	2

State	Capital Crime	Method of Execution	Number of executions after 1976	Number of executions between 1608 and 1976	Inmates on death Row as of October 2014
Nebraska	First-degree murder with a finding of at least 1 statutorily-defined aggravating circumstance	Lethal Injection	3	34	11
Nevada	First-degree murder with at least 1 of 15 aggravating circumstances	Lethal Injection	11	61	78
New Hampshire	Murder committed in the course of rape, kidnapping, drug crimes, or burglary; killing of a police officer, judge or prosecutor; murder for hire; murder by an inmate while serving a sentence of life without parole	Lethal Injection, Hanging	0	24	1
North Carolina	First-degree murder, with the finding of at least 1 of 11 statutory aggravating circumstances	Lethal Injection	43	784	160
Ohio	Aggravated murder with at least 1 of 10 aggravating circumstances	Lethal Injection	53	438	144

State	Capital Crime	Method of Execution	Number of executions after 1976	Number of executions between 1608 and 1976	Inmates on death Row as of October 2014
Oklahoma	First-degree murder in conjunction with a finding of at least 1 of 8 statutorily-defined aggravating circumstances; **rape or forcible sodomy of a victim under 14 where the defendant had a prior conviction for sexual abuse of a person under 14**	Lethal Injection, Electrocution, Firing squad – only if the above two methods are found to be unconstitutional	112	132	49
Oregon	Aggravated murder	Lethal Injection	2	122	36
Pennsylvania	First-degree murder with 18 aggravating circumstances	Lethal Injection	3	1,040	188
South Carolina	Murder with 1 of 12 aggravating circumstances; **repeat offenders of criminal sexual conduct with a minor under 11**	Lethal Injection, Electrocution	43	641	47
South Dakota	First-degree murder with 1 of 10 aggravating circumstances	Lethal Injection	3	15	3

State	Capital Crime	Method of Execution	Number of executions after 1976	Number of executions between 1608 and 1976	Inmates on death Row as of October 2014
Tennessee	First-degree murder with 1 of 16 aggravating circumstances	Lethal Injection, Electrocution	6	335	75
Texas	Criminal homicide with 1 of 9 aggravating circumstances; **second conviction for rape of a child under 14, first offense could have occurred prior to law's passage**	Lethal Injection	522	755	276
Utah	Aggravated murder	Lethal Injection, Firing squad, where the drugs for lethal injection are unavailable and if the prisoner wishes it	7	43	9
Virginia	First-degree murder with 1 of 15 aggravating circumstances	Lethal Injection, Electrocution	110	1,277	8
Washington	Aggravated first-degree murder	Lethal Injection, Hanging	5	118	9

State	Capital Crime	Method of Execution	Number of executions after 1976	Number of executions between 1608 and 1976	Inmates on death Row as of October 2014
Wyoming	First-degree murder; murder during the commission of; sexual assault, sexual abuse of a minor, arson, robbery, burglary, escape, resisting arrest, kidnapping, or abuse of a minor under 16	Lethal Injection, Gas chamber	1	22	1

The data contained in this table should not be viewed in isolation from the rest of the information presented in this document; in addition to this the reader is advised to integrate any topics discussed in this book in line with their own opinions and sentiments.

In broad terms, an aggravating factor is an instance which effectively increases the severity of the crime in question.

Text highlighted in bold applies to instances where the capital crime is not murder

Sources:

http://www.deathpenaltyinfo.org/states and-without-death-penalty

http://www.deathpenaltyinfo.org/crimes-punishable-death-penalty#BJS

http://www.deathpenaltyinfo.org/death-penalty-offenses-other-murder

http://www.deathpenaltyinfo.org/number-executions-state-and-region-1976

http://www.deathpenaltyinfo.org/documents/FactSheet.pdf

http://deathpenaltyinfo.org/executions-united-states-1608-1976-state

http://www.amnestyusa.org/our-work/issues/death-penalty/us-scheduled-executions/executions-by-state

CHAPTER 4 - METHODS OF CAPITAL PUNISHMENT IN THE UNITED STATES

The default method of execution in the United States is lethal injection and since 1977 <u>1,227 people</u> (this figure includes those executed by the US military), have been killed in this manner. Where it is available however, the inmate has the option to choose alternative methods of execution. In principle, death by lethal injection is supposed to be painless for the condemned and as stress-free as possible for the correctional officers.

- Lethal Injection:

The below procedure describes a standard three-drug protocol for capital punishment by lethal injection, and death should occur in no more than 10 minutes. The dosage of each drug administered is theoretically well above the lethal maximum required for the individual concerned, the aim is to place the inmate into a state of total unconsciousness before they die as a result of acute respiratory failure and cardiac arrest.

The condemned person is firmly restrained on to a hospital stretcher and heart monitors are attached to their body. There are always two separate hypodermic needles used, each one entered into a different vein, normally one in each arm. At this point a saline solution is intravenously fed through the needles. The prison warden then has the authority to raise the curtain allowing the execution to be viewed by the awaiting witnesses. In the US, witnesses are often given the opportunity to view the execution; these are normally close relatives of the victim/deceased.

A solution of <u>pentobarbital,</u> a strong barbiturate is then passed into the body of the inmate. *N.B. Prior to 2011 the preferred drug was sodium-thiopental; however in 2010 EU manufacturers stopped <u>exporting</u> this substance to the US. The implications of this decision are further detailed in the final chapter.* Both of these drugs however principally perform the same role, which is to depress the electrical activity of the brain, and in sufficient quantities suppress even the involuntary functions. When administered properly the injection will induce, within approximately 30 seconds, a state of unconsciousness that even prevents the sensation of pain from being detected by the brain. The hypodermic needle is then washed through with a further dose of saline solution, which serves to push any intravenously injected substance more rapidly into the circulatory system.

The next substance injected is _pancuronium bromide_ which induces muscles paralysis by inhibiting the action of the neurotransmitter _acetylcholine_ which is responsible for passing impulses throughout the nerves of the muscular system. At this stage the diaphragm ceases to function, and therefore breathing stops.

After another flush with saline solution, a chemical solution of potassium chloride is added. This induces a heart attack by upsetting the electrochemical balance of the cardiac system thus prompting a severe cardiac arrest.

Due to recent drug shortages 8 states have now opted for a one-drug protocol using a lethal dose of anesthetic, and a further 6 have plans to follow suit but have yet actually to carry out any executions in this way.

Other states continue to employ a two or three drug protocol using _midazolam_, for muscle paralysis, along with pentobarbital and vecuronium bromide; another muscle relaxant, and potassium chloride.

The botched execution of _Clayton Lockett_, convicted of double rape and the murder of one of his victims, along with _other prisoners_, have recently brought the issue of medical ethics heavily back into question. As the rules stand; doctors cannot take any part in the execution proceedings; they can only certify that the prisoner is deceased. In addition the _American Medical Association_ strongly disapproves of, and actively discourages, any doctor from participating in an execution. Furthermore the _American board of Anesthesiology_ will strike off, (disbar) any individual who plays any role in an execution. As a result of this the injection procedure itself is carried by individuals who may have little experience of using hypodermic needles. Clearly such a scenario is open to mistakes, and this has been evident for the length of time it has taken for a minority of inmates to die. In the most extreme cases the procedure has lasted for almost two hours, and whilst other cases haven't taken quite this long, they have still taken significantly longer than the target 10 minutes; in fact an _increasing number_ of problems with the lethal injection process have become apparent over recent years.

In summary, a combination of lack of experience and poor quality/inappropriate drugs has recently renewed the debate on capital punishment in general, with a particular focus on the use of the lethal injection.

The continued use of lethal injection drugs is discussed further in Chapter 7, when we outline the profound consequences these issues are threatening to have on the future of the death penalty in the United States.

- Electric Chair:

Historically, death by electrocution is the method most associated with US capital punishment. The use of the electric chair was developed to replace the practice of hanging, inherited from the British, which was viewed as inhumane. Obviously the invention and development of electric circuitry was absolutely essential to the popularity of this method.

The technique was first tested on animals, including an elephant, and from there electrocution as a form of capital punishment became the established method used in US prisons. The first person to be executed by electric chair was a convicted murderer, William Kemmler; the execution was as much an experiment as it was a method of dispensing capital justice. Two surges of direct current electricity were needed to kill the condemned, each one of which lasted over a minute. According to witnesses and newspaper reports of the time, the execution was by no means quick, humane or painless. William Kemmler was effectively roasted as the electricity passed through his body.

Approximately 4500 prisoners have been executed by electrocution, with the overwhelming majority being carried out before 1976 and only 158 since. The last person to be executed by electric Chair in the US was Robert Gleason Jr, convicted of the murder of two inmates in prison, in addition to the murder which put him in prison in the first place. Today death by electric chair is still carried out in 8 US states; although as the issues pertaining to lethal injection continue to intensify, this figure may rise in the near future.

Death by electric chair is arguably the most gruesome and painful method in which to execute a person convicted of a capital crime. The prisoner has their head and lower legs shaved; this allows for a stronger connection between the skin and electrodes, ensuring that the electrical resistance is reduced. The prisoner is then restrained with belts across the waist, ankles, wrists, arms, legs and groin. The purpose of this is to keep the prisoner as immobile as possible. A metal skull cap with electrodes and a sponge soaked in a saline solution is then placed on the head of the prisoner; the saline solution conducts electricity better than pure water. An additional electrode and saline-soaked sponge is then attached to the shaved calf of the condemned person. The prisoner is then blindfolded and a hood is placed over their head, finally on the instruction of the warden the execution procedure then begins.

An electric current only flows if the circuit in which it is carried is complete. When the execution team is satisfied that all the electrodes etc are correctly in place, the warden will give the order for the executioner to pull the switch, therefore completing the circuit. A current of between 2000 and 2500 volts is passed through the body for at least 30 seconds. This initial shock is supposed to stop the heart and induce unconsciousness within this time. Once the body has sufficiently cooled, a coroner will check to see if the prisoner can be pronounced dead. If this is not possible, the cycle is repeated until the person can be pronounced dead.

During this process the body temperature of the prisoner will exceed the boiling point of water and, as a result, the inmate is killed by a combination of suffocation, cardiac arrest and the paralysis of the nervous system. The passage of electricity through the body causes extreme physical damage to the internal organs, the eyes and the skin. The person is effectively cooked and melted. At the same time extreme spasms and gyrations occur, and the relaxation of their muscles causes defecation; for this reason prisoners are often given diapers or incontinence clothing.

As with the lethal injection, death by electrocution is supposed to be immediate but this is not always the case. There are documented cases of the combustion of the prisoner; smoke filled execution chambers; the smell of burning flesh; extreme pain being inflicted and even the execution itself being interrupted due to the malfunction of the chair or problems with the electricity supply itself. In the latter cases the prisoner is often removed, the chair repaired and cleaned and then the procedure is restarted. A succession of botched executions by electric chair is arguably the single biggest reason for the almost universal uptake of lethal injection as the primary method of carrying out capital punishment, however as we have seen a similar quandary concerning the lethal injection method is currently asserting itself on the capital states of North America.

- Gas Chamber:

Four US states; Arizona, California, Missouri and Wyoming have authorized the use of lethal gas, via a gas chamber, as a method of killing and due to the current issues obtaining the drugs necessary for the lethal injection, the state of Oklahoma is also actively considering re-authorizing its use.

This technique was first introduced by the state of Nevada in 1921, as it was considered to be a more humane method of killing those convicted of committing a capital offence. The first person to be executed in this manner was Gee Jon, a Chinese American who was convicted of the murder of the elderly relatives of a rival gang member.

By the mid-1950's, 11 states were using the gas chamber to dispense capital justice, and a total of 611 prisoners were executed in this way. All but 11 of these executions occurred before 1972, the remainder occurring after 1976, when the four-year moratorium on capital punishment ended.

The condemned person is restrained in a chair that has several holes in the seat. Underneath the chair seat is a plastic container containing sulfuric acid, crystals of sodium cyanide and distilled water. Once everyone except the condemned has left the chamber, it is pressurized and sealed, the executioner then pulls a lever. This action allows the chemical reagents to mix and, therefore, react with each other; the product is gaseous hydrogen cyanide (otherwise known as Zyklon B). Upon inhalation, hydrogen cyanide bonds very rapidly to the atoms of iron which exist in our cells. This event very rapidly inhibits the enzymes which catalyze the last stages of the oxidation of glucose inside cellular mitochondria. The result is that the supply of energy to the entire body is stopped, causing both heart and nervous system seizures. It can take several minutes for the poisoning to take effect, and if the dose of gas is not concentrated enough, the inmate does not lose consciousness. The medical profession is unequivocal in its assertions that the condemned person therefore experiences extreme pain. This position is backed up by witnesses to such executions, who state that the restrained person resists breathing for as long as possible, and then as they start to breathe in the toxic fumes, it can take several minutes for the person to lose consciousness. The pain experienced has been likened to that suffered as a result of a heart attack or drowning, which principally is exactly what gassing does to the prisoner. Ultimately, the inmate dies from hypoxia, which is the medical term for a brain starved of oxygen. Once the prisoner is pronounced dead, the room is purged of toxins by the use of exhaust fans, and the body of the deceased is sprayed with ammonia, which neutralizes the hydrogen cyanide.

- Firing Squad:

People have been executed by firing squad since the invention of the weapons themselves. However it is a comparatively rare method of execution in the United States. Since 1976 only three people have been executed by firing squad, although recent developments in the state of Utah may cause this figure to increase.

The practice was first sanctioned by the Supreme Court in 1878, and the last person to be executed in this manner was Ronnie Lee Gardner, who was sentenced in 1985 and executed in 2010. Mr. Lee was already on a murder charge when during an attempt to escape from court; he shot dead a lawyer and very nearly killed a court bailiff.

At the time of writing this book the states of Wyoming, Missouri and Virginia are debating following the example of Utah, and allowing execution by firing squad to occur if the drugs for lethal injection become unavailable.

This method arguably represents the quickest and, therefore, most humane method by which to kill a convicted capital criminal. However a firing squad is also perhaps the most 'real' of all the methods of capital punishment. When a person is shot in the manner described below, the execution is both bloody, and shines a spotlight on the fact that a prisoner has been killed by the state. This reality is a primary driver for the seeking of an alternative method such as lethal injection.

The inmate is securely bound to a chair with their head and wrists firmly in position. The prisoner is then normally blindfolded, and a black hood placed over their head. Sandbags are then placed around the chair to absorb the blood which is inevitably spilt. The heart is located by use of a stethoscope and a piece of white cloth is pinned over it, acting as a target for the firing squad. The firing squad is normally made up of five people and each rifle contains a single round, one of which will be blank. The prisoner dies due to loss of blood, rupture of the heart and respiratory failure. The prisoner loses consciousness rapidly due to the shock induced by an almost immediate stop in the supply of oxygenated blood to the brain.

- Hanging:

Prior to the invention of the electric chair, death by hanging was the primary method by which convicted persons were executed. In the United States 2718 people were hung between 1900 and 1967, and the total number of people executed by hanging since the 16th century is just shy of 10,000. The states of Delaware, New Hampshire, and Washington will execute by hanging if lethal injection is not an option, however elsewhere the practice has been superseded by the electric chair, gassing and today lethal injection.

Since 1965 three prisoners have been executed by hanging, the last being Billy Bailey in the state of Delaware in 1996. He was convicted of the double murder of an elderly couple at their farmhouse home in 1979, and he chose hanging instead of lethal injection.

The method of hanging employed today is known as the long-drop method, so called because the objective is to break the neck of the condemned person as they drop from the gallows, thus ensuring a quick death. The aim is not to strangle but to break the neck and render the person unconscious as their body shuts down and they die. In the moments before the hanging, the arms and legs of the prisoner are securely tied, they are blindfolded and/or hooded. The noose is then placed around their neck with the knot behind the left ear; this facilitates the jerking motion and thus the breaking of the neck. Furthermore, the rope itself ought to measure between 0.75 inches (1.9cm) and 1.25 inches (3.17cm) in diameter. It is also boiled and stretched so that it does not coil or lose its tension. To ensure the knot slides as the hanging takes place, it is often lubricated with an appropriate wax, soap or oil.

The drop distance which is generally between 1.5 and 3 meters, will vary from person to person. The reason is simple; each of us has a different mass, height and overall build. The procedure is practiced using a sandbag or equivalent object which has exactly the same weight (mass) as the inmate to be hung. If the length of rope is too long, the person is likely to be decapitated, if it is too short, strangulation of the condemned occurs which can take several minutes to kill.

The aim is to achieve sufficient torque when the noose jerks tight on the neck, so that it breaks instantly. If the hanging is carried out properly the drop breaks the axis neck bone, which then severs the spinal cord.

It is important to be clear that death by hanging is not instantaneous, even if the procedure is carried out properly. When the spinal cord and neck are broken, blood pressure will drop to zero in about a second and the prisoner will lose consciousness. A phenomenon known as brain death then occurs; this is when the brain is starved of blood and oxygen and therefore progressively ceases to function. Complete clinical death can, however, take up to 30 minutes to occur; however the initial breaking of the neck, when done correctly, ensures that the condemned does not experience any of this.

If the procedure does not however go to plan, a slow asphyxiation (strangulation) occurs, which is an entirely different proposition and an exceptionally painful way to die. First, compression of the carotid arteries causes the brain to swell up and form a plug on top of the spinal cord. This action causes a biological process known as the vagal reflex. The vagus nerve is one of the 12 nerves which carry impulses from the abdomen to the brain. The entire vagus system is the component of the human nervous system which controls involuntary processes such as digestion and heart rate. The vagal reflex occurs because the vagal nerves are compressed by the swelling brain and this system breaks down. The heart will stop beating, the trachea is crushed and respiratory failure ensues. Consciousness is then lost due to suffocation, and not due to the breaking of the neck and severing of the spinal cord. Strangulation is accompanied by defecation, discoloration of the skin, profound gyrating/twitching and additionally the eyes can often explode from their sockets. Death by suffocation can take up to 8 minutes.

- Summary:

Since 1976, the overwhelming majority of death row prisoners have been killed by lethal injection, however between the year 2000 and March of 2015, five prisoners have been electrocuted, and since 1977 two prisoners have been killed by firing squad, eleven in the gas chamber and three by hanging.

A total of <u>1,378 inmates</u> have been executed by all available methods since 1976.

CHAPTER 5 - THE SOCIAL ASPECTS OF CAPITAL PUNISHMENT

According to the DPIC, 72 death sentences were imposed in 2014, the lowest figure since 1976. Table two below presents the numbers broken down by individual state. When broken down by race; 43% of these inmates are white; 42% are black; 13% are Latino and 3% are Asian.

TABLE 2

State	Number of death Sentences
California	14
Florida	11
Texas	11
Alabama	4
Pennsylvania	4
Louisiana	3
North Carolina	3
Ohio	3
Arkansas	2
Oklahoma	2
Connecticut	1
Georgia	1
Indiana	1
Kentucky	1
Mississippi	1
Oregon	1
South Carolina	1
South Dakota	1

In 2013 the number of capital punishment sentences passed was 79, and although the numbers differ, the overall racial breakdown is broadly similar. However in 2012, there were a total of 77 death sentences imposed but the racial breakdown was 41% black, 39% white, with the remainder being 19% Latino and 3% other backgrounds. Whilst it is beyond the scope of this text to analyze these breakdowns in any comprehensive detail, several broad assertions can be stated:

- According to Amnesty, in the USA most death row inmates are on death row for capital offences against white victims
- Overall, irrespective of their color a defendant is "several times" more likely to be sentenced to death if the victim was white.
- Research consistently points to the reality that race is, therefore, a driving factor in capital crimes.
- African Americans are more likely to be sentenced to death, particularly in regions where all white juries are common place.
- According to the DPIC, 80% of people executed since 1976 have been involved in crimes concerning white victims, this is set against a backdrop where half of all murder victims are African American.
- Overall African American defendants are 3 times as likely to receive the death penalty compared to their white counterparts.
- According to the 2013 US census, approximately 78% of the US population is white, approximately 13% are black, 17% are Latino and 5% are Asian.

Figures such as these unsurprisingly encourage ideas and suggestions that a racial bias exists in the US capital crime litigation system. The issue of race has not been ignored by the Supreme Court. In 1986 it was ruled that any prosecutor who attempts to alter a jury in such a way that there is a resulting racial imbalance, is compelled to present good cause for doing so. However, despite statistical evidence to the contrary, in 1987 the same institution also ruled that the only mechanism by which racial imbalance in a jury could be deemed unconstitutional, was if there was clear intent to employ racism against a capital defendant.

Perhaps unsurprisingly there is a profound gender disparity in US executions. The first woman to be executed in the US was Jane Champion in 1632, in the state of Virginia, and although it is absolutely beyond the remit of this text to explore this issue in any great detail, the figures do make stark reading:

- Since 1976, only 14 of the total number of executions have been women.
- Of the 8,375 capital punishment sentences imposed, only 178 have been women.
- Women only constitute 2% of the total death row prison population.

One factor behind the disparity is a perceived reluctance on the part of the judiciary to sanction the execution of women, irrespective of their ethnic background. However it is also true that women do not commit anything like the amounts of first degree and aggravated murder offences, which are considered capital offences. Practically all women on death row are there because they have killed spouses/partners, family members or children, or have killed in response to sustained domestic violence. For cultural reasons there is a tendency to pass less harsh sentences for such crimes.

Intertwined with this is the notion; according to academics such as Elizabeth Rapaport (Professor of law at the University of New Mexico), that women are more likely to commit such crimes due to an emotional response or anger, as opposed to men who are more likely to commit pre-meditated and planned murder. In addition, in general terms women tend to possess different prior criminal histories, if indeed they even have a criminal record. Men are statistically more likely to have a past criminal history which often results in the imposition of a capital sentence. How such factors will come to influence the debate on capital punishment in the future remains to be seen.

- Clemency:

An act of clemency is basically a show of mercy or leniency to a prisoner, in a legal framework the power to give clemency rests with an official of the state or government, this can include the president.

The 32 states which impose capital punishment, must go through a comprehensive process known as a 'clemency review' before capital punishment is actually carried out. Time scales can vary but overall the review must occur several weeks before the scheduled execution date, and the condemned themselves are entitled to request a formal meeting (interview) with the parole board. The prisoner is not however entitled to legal representation at this meeting.

The DPIC records that since 1976; fewer than 300 death row prisoners have been accorded clemency. Although framed as humanitarian, the reasoning is more to do with both the validity and appropriateness of the conviction itself.

For example George Ryan, who in 2002 was the outgoing state governor of Illinois, had by 2003 given clemency to all 160 death row prisoners, despite the doubtless fierce and heartbreaking testimonies of the victims' relatives. It was decided that the convictions were unsound, including the alleged use of torture to produce confessions. All the death sentences were commuted to life imprisonment; in fact four inmates were actually fully pardoned.

Table 3 below shows the numbers of prisoners, by state, that have been granted clemency since 1976.

TABLE 3

State clemencies since 1976	Number of clemencies
Illinois	187
Ohio	19
Georgia	9
Virginia	8
New Jersey	8
Florida	6
Maryland	6
New Mexico	5
South Carolina	5
Oklahoma	4
Indiana	3
Tennessee	3
Missouri	3
Kentucky	2
Louisiana	2
Texas	2
Alabama	1
Arkansas	1
Delaware	1
Idaho	1
Montana	1
Nevada	1
Federal	1
Total	**279**

- Commuting sentences:

In the US, if a capital punishment is commuted the result is generally that the prisoner is then sentenced to life without parole. Such an eventuality is not a pardon because the prisoner is still considered guilty of the crime in question; it is just the sentence that has been made less severe (depending on your point of view). As with clemency the authority to commute a capital punishment in this manner resides with the relevant authorities.

Overall, as part of the conditions of the reinstatement of capital punishment in 1976, the capital states must have statute protocols, which allow for the commuting of capital punishment to life imprisonment. According to research carried out by the DPIC, the level of support for the death penalty becomes significantly less than its current level if respondents can be sure that a long (if not life-long) prison term will be served by a convicted prisoner. In short, if jurors and the public at large are aware that a murderer or child killer will be sentenced to a minimum of multiple decades in prison, with no possibility of parole, the conviction is sound and the family of the victim is compensated, then support for capital punishment drops to 41%. At the same time, if such an alternative sanction does not exist, then support for capital punishment surges to over 70%. This facet of the death penalty debate, i.e. the sentencing, is a key driver in the campaigning of activists who oppose capital punishment. Intertwined with this position, is the reality of prisoner exonerations, i.e. being found innocence, for the capital crimes for which they were convicted. The DPIC states that since 1973, 150 inmates on death row have at a later date been proved innocent of all charges; with new forensic/DNA evidence being a contributing factor in establishing the innocence of 20 of these prisoners. The current rate of prisoner exonerations is presently running at about 5 prisoners per year.

- Mental Illness:

A further complication when discussing capital punishment is the mental state of the convicted person. This is again a hugely complex area and therefore cannot be explained in great detail in the body of this text, however it can be asserted that mental illness is not unique to prisoners on death row; there are hundreds of thousands of mentally ill prisoners in the United States, and the debate about whether they should be incarcerated is again not the subject of this eBook.

A mental illness is loosely defined as any condition which disrupts the normal behavioral, emotional or conscious functioning of an individual. Such disruptions have no single cause, and are rooted in the complex psychological debates concerning the relative roles of 'nature and nurture', and their influence on the personality.

In the US any prisoner who is deemed insane, in the sense that they cannot tell right from wrong, i.e. don't understand why they are being prosecuted in the first place, or what may happen to them, or why, are considered to be mentally retarded and therefore cannot be executed.

In 1986 the Supreme Court added 'mental competency stipulations' to all capital cases:

- If therapy can later restore the prisoner's competency, then they can be executed if the offence is a designated capital crime.
- Any person who is considered mentally ill but not retarded or indeed insane can be executed.

According to the Non-Governmental Organization - Mental Health America, the numbers of mentally ill people on death row is <u>steadily increasing</u>.

Since the 1980's at least <u>60 prisoners</u> have been executed who were considered to have a mental health issue, in fact between <u>5% and 10%</u> of the current death row population have some kind of equivalent problem. <u>Polls</u> in the US suggest that twice as many people oppose capital punishment for mentally ill people as support it.

- Minors and Juveniles

The final factor is the question of minors and juveniles on death row, and those who were within this age group when the capital offence was committed.

In 1642 <u>Thomas Graunger</u> became the first juvenile to be executed in the United States. His crime was multiple incidences of bestiality and he was hung in the colony of Plymouth, in the state of Massachusetts; he was no more than 17 years old.

Since the 17th century, roughly 365 prisoners have been executed for crimes committed when they were juveniles, approximately 2% of the total, and since Capital punishment was reinstated in 1976, 22 juvenile prisoners have been executed. All of these prisoners were juveniles (16-17 years old) when the crimes were committed, but adults when they were executed; over half of these were executed in <u>Texas</u>. Under the auspices of the provisions of treaties, such as the UN convention on the '<u>rights of the child</u>', the execution of children is prohibited; however since 1990 seven countries, including the US have executed children. Furthermore the US is still yet to formally <u>ratify</u> the 'rights of a child' convention, the only other country not to have done this yet is Somalia. There has however been some progress in this matter due to interventions by the Supreme Court. In 1988 following a vote on the subject, a result of <u>5-3 in favor,</u> agreed that the execution of offenders, who were 15 years old or younger when they committed the crime, was unconstitutional. In fact since the start of 2015; no capital state can execute a prisoner if the crime was committed when the offender was 18 years old or younger.

- Summary:

Taken collectively, the above considerations ought to underpin any discussion on capital punishment, whether it is in the US or elsewhere. In essence these are the foundations of any debate on the value of capital punishment, and as such need to be framed within the points raised in the next chapter.

Sources

http://deathpenaltyinfo.org/2014-sentencing#2014inmates

http://deathpenaltyinfo.org/2013-sentencing

http://www.deathpenaltyinfo.org/2012-sentencing

http://www.amnestyusa.org/our-work/issues/death-penalty/us-death-penalty-facts/death-penalty-and-race

http://www.deathpenaltyinfo.org/race-and-death-penalty

http://quickfacts.census.gov/qfd/states/00000.html

http://www.jstor.org/discover/10.2307/490783?sid=21105694564341&uid=37380 32&uid=2&uid=70&uid=4&uid=2129

http://campbelllawobserver.com/2014/03/executions-in-the-modern-era-women-on-death-row-and-gender-bias-concerns/

http://www.deathpenaltyinfo.org/clemency

http://www.deathpenaltyinfo.org/innocence-list-those-freed-death-row

http://www.deathpenaltyinfo.org/sentencing-life-americans-embrace-alternatives-death-penalty

http://www.mentalhealthamerica.net/

http://www.huffingtonpost.com/sean-mcelwee/abolish-death-penalty_b_3557782.html

CHAPTER 6 - ARGUMENTS FOR AND AGAINST CAPITAL PUNISHMENT

Without a doubt, any discussion about capital punishment is by its very nature going to be emotive, if not acrimonious. The debate has been going on for centuries and for as long as it continues to exist as a form of sentencing; it will obviously continue to do so. It is as much an ethical and moral question, as it is a question of deterrence and legality. In short; does the state have the right to take the life of a prisoner, found guilty of murder or another designated equivalent offence, or is this type of retribution wholly unacceptable under any circumstances? From a deterrent perspective, the obvious question to ask is whether the prospect of their own death will deter an individual from carrying out the offence, or is the prospect of a lifetime of incarceration a greater discouragement? From a psychological perspective, one has to ask whether such questions are even present in the mind of a person who perpetrates such extreme crimes. For the deterrent argument to be valid there must be evidence that in states where the death penalty exists, the incidence of capital offences committed in those areas is lower than in areas where capital punishment does not exist. The numbers of authoritative studies which assert that capital punishment is effective; are as plentiful and passionate as those that hold the opposite view. In fact the actual results suggest that the prospect of death for a capital crime makes no difference to overall capital crime statistics at all.

It is important to remember that any discussion on the death penalty resides firmly in the domain of social science, and as such it is almost impossible in any definitive sense, to assert that any correlations between the level of deterrent and the number of incidences are ever in existence.

It's important to reiterate the above statement because for many supporters of capital punishment, deterrence is not the driving force. They are often far more focused on the retribution angle, and the satisfaction it is seen to deliver to the families and relatives of the victims of the most serious crimes. When we hear of the most heinous crimes, it sometimes seems that capital punishment is the only answer. For example; when we hear about the <u>gang rape</u>, beating, biting, mutilation and murder of women in <u>India</u> and other parts of the world, from an emotional perspective it becomes very difficult to argue against capital punishment. In a recent case the assailants of a gang rape repeatedly penetrated the sexual organs of the victim with such force that they were able to pull her intestines out through her vagina; she died in hospital a few days later. When you hear stories like this it becomes very difficult to imagine losing any sleep over the hanging sentences which will be carried out if the perpetrators, having already confessed, are actually convicted.

Despite the undisputed horror of crimes such as these, which sadly are not isolated, the counter argument still exists that the sanctity of human life overrides any considerations of satisfaction and/or retribution.

Other aspects of this debate focus on the credibility of evidence and in turn the trust we have in law enforcement agencies, raising the appalling possibility of a double injustice that can occur following the execution of an innocent person. Additionally there is the issue of discrimination based on race, class and gender that was discussed in Chapter 4. In actual fact, in the UK cases of the Guildford Four and the Birmingham Six, the nationality of the accused was a fundamental reason for their conviction, and when all these factors are considered there have been a minimum of 150 equivalent examples of similar injustices in the US.

So, is the death penalty a deterrent? The short answer to this question based on empirical evidence, is that it is not. According to Amnesty, based on FBI data, in 2008 all states without a death penalty statute had a murder rate which did not exceed the national murder average. Furthermore, in 2009 a study demonstrated the almost universal position on the part of US criminologists, that the prospect of capital punishment does not deter the committing of a capital crime when measured against the deterrent value of a lengthy prison term. There is in fact more than anecdotal evidence that in states where the death penalty does exist, the murder rate of is no lower than in states where it does not, in fact between the years 2000 and 2010, the murder rate in states with capital punishment was anything from 25-46% higher than in states without capital punishment. A more recent report published in 2012 based on over 30 years of primary research concluded that studies supporting the deterrent position are scientifically unsound and cannot be used to inform debate on capital punishment. Overall, evidence suggests that the presence of a death penalty in a state fails to decrease the murder rate. Murder rates although astoundingly high, are in a constant state of flux and overall in the US they are currently lower than in previous years.

Those who support capital punishment from a deterrent perspective seem to ignore these statistics, as well as the apparent evidence of racially biased. Using deterrence as a justification for capital punishment just doesn't stand up to scrutiny when capital states are still reporting high murder figures, in fact of the 25 states with the highest murder rates, only three of them (Alaska, Michigan and New York) don't have capital statutes. It can therefore fairly confidently be said that capital punishment has not acted as a deterrent to violent crime in North America.

This view is increasingly being aired by those who are on the front line of law enforcement, i.e. the police force. The police force in fact rank the presence of the death penalty, as the least of all effective mechanisms by which to prevent crime, in fact it is significantly superseded by notions of increasing the number of police officers on the street, increasing employment opportunities and reducing substance abuse.

Arguably of equal importance to this debate, is the cost of the implementation of capital punishment. For opponents of the death penalty the argument is obvious, if the practice is not a deterrent then the question of the allocation of financial resources must be considered.

According to the Guardian newspaper it costs an average of $300 Million to execute a death row prisoner in California. Over $4Billion dollars has been spent on administering capital punishment in California since 1978. Such figures are not isolated or extreme when it comes to the financing of the death penalty across capital states, in fact:

- The state of Maryland spent $186Million executing 5 prisoners; since then the state has abolished capital punishment.
- The state of Texas is spending $2.3 million per death row prisoner and has roughly 300 capital prisoners awaiting execution.

It is therefore reasonable to believe that a similar financial outlay is necessary for the approximate 3000 prisoners imprisoned across the US in exactly the same position. It is not just the cost of the execution that is excessive, it is also the cost of incarceration (particularly when you consider that some inmates have been on death row for a number of decades), the appeals process, additional trials, and the requirement for specialist lawyers that begs the question, "could the resources be better spent on crime prevention?"

For supporters of the death penalty the answer is obvious; the whole process should be streamlined, thus decreasing the financial burden and accelerating the rate at which executions take place. In Chapter 7 we will show that this strategy is essentially impossible.

The current situation in the United States is that the death penalty is funded at the state level through taxation, and as such does divert financial resources from other crime controlling initiatives. This is one of the reasons why not every state employs the death penalty.

Another rather clinical question that we must ask is "does it cost more to execute a prisoner or to incarcerate them for the remainder of their life?" A survey reported on the DPIC website suggests that on average it costs $1million more to prosecute capital trials than non-capital trials, and that as a result in the case of Washington State where capital punishment was reinstated in 1981, the death penalty has cost $120 million, as since then 5 death row inmates have been executed.

In these austere times it would be irresponsible to ignore such economic realities, particularly since the global recession has caused savage cuts across all sectors of the economy, including law enforcement. The result has been the early release of prisoners, who then subsequently re-offended and the redundancy of thousands of prison and police officers across North America. Such decisions are being taken by states that continue to invest millions of dollars into a capital punishment programme which offers no demonstrable reduction in the incidence of capital crime.

In addition the time taken for a condemned prisoner to be put to death has increased markedly over the years, from approximately 6 years in 1985 to over 15 years at the time of writing this in 2015. Irrespective of issues raised in the next chapter, the overall rate of executions is actually slowly decreasing. This means it is less likely that capital prisoners will actually ever be executed; in fact the current probability of execution can be calculated at 1 in 72. The paradox here is that a scenario has evolved whereby death row prisoners are in effect more likely to serve a life without parole sentence but in the more severe and costly conditions of a death row section of a prison. A significant numbers of lawyers have over the years argued that imprisonment on death row is both a cruel and an unusual punishment.

Such strong assertions present the fundamental question; why do 32 states in North America still have capital punishment on their statutes? The US emphasises the autonomy of different states and the death penalty is administered on a state by state basis, for supporters of the death penalty, who are still the majority, capital punishment is a deeply rooted component of US frontier and pioneer history, and as such is part of their national identity or character.

There is also the belief amongst supporters of capital punishment that "an eye for an eye" is the best method of dispensing justice. Putting this in very simple terms; if you kill, the state has the right to take your life in return. If you hold this belief, any notions of mitigating or extenuating circumstances, as well as any kind of empathy for capital prisoners, or concern for outside/international opinions, become irrelevant. Opponents would of course disagree with such subjective notions.

It can be argued that the case against the death penalty is stronger today than it has ever been, however it would be a mistake to believe that this in any way means that capital punishment is on its way out in the US.

CHAPTER 7 - THE FUTURE OF THE DEATH PENALTY IN THE UNITED STATES

Prior to 2010, sodium thiopental was the key anesthetic drug used to carry out lethal injections. The drug is no longer manufactured in the United States, and in November 2010 the UK became the last European nation to ban the export of sodium thiopental to the US, followed in 2011 by a de-facto embargo on the export of lethal injection drugs from the EU to the US. Provisions of the European human rights act dictate that while a country is signatory to the act, it cannot under any circumstances execute a prisoner. In line with this it was consequently ruled that the export of the drugs used to carry out capital punishment by intravenous injection, was therefore illegal. To emphasize this point further, in March 2011 the state of Georgia had its stockpiles of sodium thiopental confiscated by the DEA. The principle reasons for the seizure being over the legality of the imported consignment and whether the chemicals "4 year use by date" had expired. At around the same time Arkansas acquired the drug and then passed supplies on to the states of Mississippi, Tennessee and Oklahoma. Such practices apparently contravene state law and free trade restrictions. The state of Kentucky avoided similar action from the DEA, by surrendering its stockpiles of sodium thiopental later in the same year. In addition small scale manufacturers of equivalent drugs have all but ceased the export of lethal injection drugs to the US. In fact an Indian based company called Kayem Pharmaceuticals also stopped exporting sodium thiopental to the US in 2011.

To further complicate matters; in June 2011 the Danish pharmaceutical company Lundbeck stated that they would restrict the sale and manufacture of pentobarbital. Lundbeck was the only licensed manufacturer and distributor of pentobarbital in the US. Proponents of capital punishment in the US can expect such actions to continue in line with EU commitments to a global cessation of capital punishment. For example, when in 2012 Missouri announced it would follow a single injection protocol using propofol, a strong anesthetic, the UK banned the export of the drug to the US where it is used in general medical care. In the face of an EU-wide export ban the Missouri decision was reversed on the orders of the state governor.

According to Richard Dieter of the Death Penalty Information Centre, "The EU embargo has slowed down but not stopped executions, it has made states seem somewhat desperate and not in control, putting the death penalty in a negative light, with an uncertain future".

These changes have meant that for states which allow the death penalty, their only option is either to revert to previous methods of execution, or to experiment effectively with unknown formulas and mixtures of lethal injection drugs. This is the context in which the future of capital punishment finds itself and in this chapter we will try to examine the consequences and possible future outcomes this situation is likely to have.

Since 2011 the whole procurement process for lethal injection drugs has become shrouded in secrecy and in fact some states are now under no legal obligation to reveal the source of the drugs they use to kill their death row prisoners. The required stockpiles to carry out the executions are therefore now being acquired via clandestine means. In addition it would appear that since the decision of the Hospira pharmaceutical company to stop the manufacture of sodium thiopental, an invisible college has emerged to ensure the availability of dwindling stockpiles. The reason for this in the opinion of the supporters of capital punishment, is to protect any suppliers of an execution drug by keeping them out of the public domain and therefore away from any harassment from anti-death penalty activists. If this secrecy concerning executions can be maintained, then it becomes harder for opponents of capital punishment to stop them. However, openness and transparency are supposed to be the hallmarks of any democracy and as a result should therefore theoretically apply to most of the United States. As a citizen the obvious question is therefore "if state officials are behaving with much secrecy in regards to their execution protocols, what else are they hiding?"

The resulting current situation for lethal injections is that the drugs being used are; untested; insufficiently regulated; improperly sourced; administered by untrained personnel and have no definite lethal minimum dose set. This is all as a consequence of a miss-managed procurement policy and is best explained by referencing some real examples.

The executions of both Clayton Lockett and Charles Warner (convicted of the sexual assault and murder of an 11-month-old infant girl), were carried out in January 2015 with an untested cocktail of drugs. It took 43 minutes for Clayton Locket to die and 18 for Charles Warner. Lethal injection is supposed to be quick, effective and humane. The issues raised by such occurrences strike at the heart of the whole death penalty debate. A further complication with the Lockett / Warner execution was that the republican governor of Oklahoma, Mary Fallin, authorized the executions even though there was an agreement with the Supreme Court to stay the executions for legal reasons. At the time the concoction used in the Lockett execution had only been used once before in Florida, but in doses which exceed those used in Oklahoma by a factor of five. The Oklahoma state investigation into the death of Clayton Lockett concluded that prison staff failed intravenously to inject the drugs (i.e. they missed the veins). In response the procedures have been altered (i.e. the executioners have been trained) and the dose of drugs used increased significantly.

In 2014 the state of Oklahoma executed its 192nd death row inmate, <u>Michael Lee Wilson</u>, (<u>convicted</u> of robbery and first degree murder), by injection with pentobarbital. This substance is widely seen as a substitute for sodium thiopental but it is not well regulated and if contaminated will result in excruciating pain even if injected properly. According to witnesses and those carrying out the execution of Mr. Wilson, he called out; "I feel like my whole body is burning" during the procedure.

In the absence of established verified protocols for the use of the lethal injection drugs, the inmates are themselves the de-facto subjects of trial and error experimentation. For instance after the Wilson execution, the state of Ohio executed <u>Dennis McGuire</u> in January 2014 with the then untried drug cocktail of midazolam and an opiate called hydromorphone. It took 20 minutes for him to die.

The above cases are by no means isolated; in fact since 1982 approximately <u>45 executions</u> have been botched, with the majority occurring as a result of poor lethal injection protocols.

For supporters of capital punishment this is merely the symptom of a need to overhaul the whole lethal injection process. They contend that the overwhelming majority of executions proceed as intended, and that they are a quick, efficient and humane way of killing an inmate convicted of a capital offence. They would cite examples such as <u>Johnny Shane Kormondy</u> who was convicted of murder and multiple rapes in 1993. He was pronounced dead "shortly" after the administration of the same drug cocktail injected into Charles Warner. In other words the procedure fulfilled its basic constitutional requirements. Further examples of successful executions include the case of Michael Worthington who was convicted of raping and murdering his neighbor and was executed in July 2014.

Overall <u>primary research</u> from the US suggests that from the period 1890 to 2010 the total percentage of bungled or botched executions was approximately only 7%, and for lethal injections the figure was about 3%. It must be stressed that these results do not include the current figures for unsuccessful executions. Lawyers for the state of Oklahoma assert that there is no evidence that midazolam would be ineffective and they also point out that the 10 executions prior to that of Clayton Lockett proceeded without incident and were therefore a success. Additionally they declare that opponents can only use the minority of cases, such as Clayton Lockett and Charles Warner when trying to prove that the mal-administration of drugs is in fact even a concern.

From a supporters perspective this is all well and good but it is difficult to see how the current position is tenable. In short, to even casual observers there are simply too many mistakes occurring for the current situation to remain unchanged. Put succinctly; if the executions cannot demonstrably be carried out professionally, with transparency, openness and with all the legally binding standards met, then the whole notion of capital punishment must be called into question.

A further issue for supporters of capital punishment is that if the steady stream of botched executions continues, their case can only become weaker. Such realities are a key driver behind the desire of supporters of capital punishment, for capital states to reform the whole lethal injection process.

Other advocates of capital punishment suggest that the practice should be discontinued and alternative methods sought, in practical terms this would be likely to mean a return to post 1977 methods. The use of alternative methods, even if previously proven is difficult to justify, after all wasn't the whole point of superseding the electric chair with the lethal injection, to demonstrate a higher level of humanity? Indeed, it could be argued that if the lethal injection is no longer humane or effective, then there is no replacement for it? In this instance, the quagmire of debate around capital punishment in the US will only become more viscous.

The European factor cannot be ignored or understated; as a group of nations the EU extols the virtues of a world which is free from capital punishment. Moreover it is not unheard of for representatives of various EU countries, to attempt to influence death penalty decisions in the US by directly contacting those involved in the decision to execute capital offenders. Additionally, it is not unheard of for organizations within the EU to personally fund the anti-death penalty groups within the United States. The European nations are also particularly vocal in their condemnation of the use of a capital sentence on individuals who were minors when the crime took place. Charges of hypocrisy have however been levied against the EU due to its policy on Iran and other nations which also have the death penalty.

The Supreme Court is currently reviewing the use of lethal injection drugs, i.e. the judges are deliberating on whether death by lethal injection in its current form constitutes cruel and unusual punishment. Various cases will be heard in April and a decision is expected by July 2015 at the latest. This is the first time since 2008 that the Supreme Court has investigated the use of the lethal injection, in 2008 the vote was (7-2) in favor of the lethal injection and of the injection protocols then in existence (the same protocols that exist today).

According to opponents of the death penalty, midazolam is not regulated by the FDA (at least as an anesthetic) and as such there is no standard protocol for its use in administering capital punishment. As the first of the three drugs to be administered in the three-drug protocol described in chapter 4 it is supposed to render the inmate unconscious. Failure to achieve this results in unnecessary pain and suffering during the next stages of the procedure. Arguably the execution of Joseph Wood in August 2014 by the State of Arizona, presents the most profound example of a bungled execution. Mr. Wood was convicted in 1989 of the double murder of his then partner and her father. The prisoner was injected with a cocktail of drugs which exceeded the minimum set down by the Arizona prison authorities by a factor of 15; however it still took two hours for the inmate to die. The lawyers for the deceased made it apparent that they were concerned about both the potency and sourcing of the drugs employed to carry out the sentence, and when it takes two hours and 15 injections of a given drug concoction to kill a person, such fundamental questions are not simply going to disappear. The added complication of this particular case was that despite concerted efforts on the part the defendant's lawyers and federal judges, the execution was in fact authorized by the Supreme Court.

In the face of these issues, particularly where the supplies of lethal injection drugs are concerned, Capital states are increasingly opting for previous methods of execution. Currently some states such as Nebraska have no legal means by which to carry out capital punishment, whilst other states such as Utah, Wyoming and Tennessee, have voted to either re-employ the firing squad and electric chair, or are in the process of considering doing so.

At present and pending a ruling by the Supreme Court, executions in Ohio are effectively temporarily suspended. The same is not true of Florida which has no plans to interrupt its execution schedule, and is the only US state which is carrying on irrespective of the deliberations of the Supreme Court. Furthermore, Florida has no plans to find an alternative execution protocol. In 2014 the Florida department of corrections executed 8 inmates by employing a 3 drug protocol, using midazolam as the anesthetic.

It is important to stress that the prisoners incarcerated on death row are, assuming safe convictions, guilty of terrible crimes. The question is whether the use of the lethal injection in its current form contravenes the eighth amendment, due to the possible inefficiencies of midazolam.

As it stands, the overwhelming majority of executions are taking place in Texas, Florida, Oklahoma, Missouri, Ohio and Arizona, although the dynamics of the debate regarding midazolam arguably do not apply to Texas and Missouri as they do not use it for their lethal injection protocols. Their preference is for a massive injection of pentobarbital, either singularly or in combination with other heart-stopping drugs such as potassium chloride. Whilst the Supreme Court deliberates, the next 3 scheduled executions in Oklahoma have been temporarily halted.

In 2014 the Supreme Court also ruled that the margin of error applied to IQ tests must be increased, meaning that people with mental issues are likely to be executed less often.

A number of cases in Missouri have recently been referred back to the state for specific legal reasons concerning appeal deadlines, as well as those pertaining to a possible mental condition and therefore the ability of individuals to avoid cruel and unusual punishment. As part of this investigation, the Missouri department of corrections may also be compelled to reveal how it procures its death penalty drugs.

Overall the replacement drugs, particularly those for sodium thiopental, fall outside the remit of FDA regulations both in terms of their composition, and the degree to which different cocktails of drugs are effective. In other words the concoctions employed are untested and unregulated. Prior to the current shortage of lethal injection drugs, practically every execution across the US was carried out using the same three-drug protocol. There is also the issue surrounding the fact that the injections are still being administered by people with almost no medical training, making the potential for mistakes in administering the punishment obvious. There is more than anecdotal evidence that members of execution teams have a bare minimum of medical training before carrying out executions. Indeed the post mortem (autopsy) of Clayton Lockett asserts that a catalogue of errors caused by poor training was the fundamental cause of the fouled up execution. It is not difficult to see why Georgia (which uses a one-drug protocol) has as of March 2015, temporarily ceased all scheduled executions until these issues are resolved.

CONCLUSION

Public support for the death penalty in the US has ebbed and flowed for decades and will likely do so for the foreseeable future. Murder is the principal capital crime in the United States however for particularly horrific crimes involving the abuse of children; some states will seek a capital conviction. As of March 2015 approximately 3350 inmates are incarcerated in death row, of these two are for offences which do not involve the death of the victim.

The use of the death penalty has been in steady decline since the turn of the 21st century, recently the principal reason for the decline in executions has been due to the unavailability of the drugs required to carry out lethal injections. There is also a growing preference amongst the US public for life without parole sentences, which has developed out of concern over the validity of certain convictions. There has been a definite gravitation toward life sentencing and away from capital punishment. From a social science perspective, the implication is that if the prosecution, judges, jury and the relatives of victims are assured that the convicted prisoner will die in prison, they are less likely to demand the ultimate sanction.

If one takes an objective look at the facts concerning the economics and effectiveness of the death penalty, then one can argue that it no longer has a purpose; however from a subjective and emotional perspective, it becomes difficult to argue against capital punishment on these facts alone. For opponents of capital punishment it becomes very difficult to say to a grieving family of a victim of a vile crime, that they are not entitled to retributive justice. It is in this context that states which carry out the death penalty have been obliged to either come up with alternative drugs, or revert to previous methods of execution; namely hanging; firing squad and most commonly the electric chair, in order to be able to continue administrating capital punishment.

All of these discussions are occurring at a time when:

- Capital punishment is at its lowest point in US history, with an average of 71 executions being carried out each year between 1995 and 2005 and only 44 a year between 2006 and 2013.

- There is effectively a moratorium until July 2015 on all executions in the US, with the exception of Florida and California. This is expected to stay in place until the Supreme Court completes its review of lethal injection drugs.

It remains to be seen what the future holds for capital punishment in the US.

FURTHER SOURCES

http://deathpenalty.procon.org/view.resource.php?resourceID=001769

http://www.theguardian.com/world/capital-punishment

http://www.amnestyusa.org/our-work/issues/death-penalty

http://www.amnestyusa.org/our-work/issues/death-penalty/us-death-penalty-facts/death-penalty-and-innocence

http://www.bbc.co.uk/ethics/capitalpunishment/

http://www.deathpenaltyinfo.org/methods-execution?scid=8&did=245#state

http://www.washingtonpost.com/blogs/govbeat/wp/2014/04/30/map-how-each-state-chooses-to-execute-its-death-row-inmates/

http://journalstar.com/news/state-and-regional/nebraska/report-grim-future-for-u-s-death-penalty/article_23b26357-55ae-5835-98fb-a38f7a70e331.html

http://www.pewforum.org/2007/12/19/an-impassioned-debate-an-overview-of-the-death-penalty-in-america/

http://www.jstor.org/discover/10.2307/41299271?sid=21105610762681&uid=2&uid=4&uid=3738032&uid=2129&uid=70

http://www.jstor.org/discover/10.2307/4246865?sid=21105610762681&uid=4&uid=70&uid=2&uid=3738032&uid=2129

http://criminal.findlaw.com/criminal-procedure/the-u-s-and-the-death-penalty.html

http://progressiveproselytizing.blogspot.co.uk/2011/01/on-death-penalty-question-of-objectives.html

http://www.nytimes.com/1999/11/18/us/florida-s-messy-executions-put-the-electric-chair-on-trial.html?src=pm&pagewanted=1

http://www.capitalpunishmentuk.org/chair.html

http://www.washingtonpost.com/blogs/the-fix/wp/2015/03/11/why-firing-squads-might-become-more-common-in-the-u-s/

http://www.bbc.co.uk/news/magazine-27303555

http://www.washingtonpost.com/blogs/worldviews/wp/2014/04/30/4-horrible-forms-of-capital-punishment-more-humane-than-oklahomas-botched-execution/

http://www.theatlantic.com/politics/archive/2015/03/utah-may-bring-the-firing-squad-back/387442/

http://time.com/3742818/utah-firing-squad-execution-lethal-injection/

http://www.washingtonpost.com/news/post-nation/wp/2014/05/01/everything-you-need-to-know-about-executions-in-the-united-states/

http://www.capitalpunishmentuk.org/hanging.html

http://www.theguardian.com/film/2015/mar/01/indias-daughter-documentary-rape-delhi-women-indian-men-attitudes

http://www.nytimes.com/interactive/2011/04/11/us/20110411_LETHAL_DOCS.html?action=click&contentCollection=U.S.&module=RelatedCoverage&region=Marginalia&pgtype=article

http://www.motherjones.com/mojo/2014/06/autopsy-clayton-lockett-botched-execution-oklahoma

http://www.huffingtonpost.co.uk/2014/08/13/ukip-mep-louise-bours-wants-to-bring-back-the-death-penalty_n_5674273.html

http://www.economist.com/news/united-states/21601270-america-falling-out-love-needle-slow-death-death-penalty

https://www.aclu.org/capital-punishment/death-penalty-101

http://campbelllawobserver.com/2014/03/executions-in-the-modern-era-women-on-death-row-and-gender-bias-concerns/

http://www.bbc.co.uk/ethics/capitalpunishment/

http://america.aljazeera.com/articles/2014/4/8/mental-illness-prison.html

http://www.canadiancrc.com/UN_CRC/US_position_UN_Convention_Rights_of_Child.aspx

http://www.deathpenaltyinfo.org/sentencing-life-americans-embrace-alternatives-death-penalty

http://www.daytondailynews.com/news/news/crime-law/death-penalty-not-efficient-police-chiefs-say/nM5kg/

http://www.economist.com/news/united-states/21608773-judge-strikes-blow-against-capital-punishment-cruel-and-unusual

http://www.texasobserver.org/solitary-men/